# How to Fix Yourself
# For Good
# Lose the Weight
# For Women

Kathy Lindert, C.Ht., C.I.

Your Favorite Hypnotist!

www.advancedhypno.com

Title ID: 4543310
ISBN-13:978-1494285579

# DEDICATION

This book is dedicated to all the people who have taught me the art of hypnosis and shown me that there is no stopping a person who is ready to achieve a goal!

A special thanks to my husband who has supported me and my dreams.

To all my Weight Loss Clients, thank you, you are now helping others succeed!

To the National Guild of Hypnotists – for having great speakers and classes that have shown me how to be the best I can be.

To all the pioneers of hypnosis and to the hypnotists now that continue to find new ways to help people succeed.  Thank you.

Portrait by Nandita Bery Photography

Cover design by www.uniquedesignz.net

# CONTENTS

# WHY WEIGHT LOSS FOR WOMEN?

FOR MANY OF THE CLIENTS THAT COME TO SEE ME, I AM THE LAST RESORT. I AM OKAY WITH THAT BECAUSE I LOOK FORWARD TO TEACHING THEM THE WAY TO LIVE!

WOMEN USE FOOD FOR SO MANY DIFFERENT REASONS. WE USE IT BECAUSE WE ARE SAD, HAPPY, ANGRY, STRESSED, OR AS A COMPANION TO HELP US THROUGH OUR DAY. WOMEN ALSO USE FOOD TO GET TOGETHER WITH OTHER WOMEN AND TALK. FOOD IS AN EXCUSE FOR SO MANY THINGS THAT WOMEN HAVE FORGOTTEN THE REAL PURPOSE OF FOOD.

WOMEN DO NOT USE FOOD AS IT IS INTENDED TO BE USED---AS FUEL! FOOD IS FUEL FOR OUR BODIES. HOWEVER, WE HAVE BEEN TRAINED---YES, TRAINED---TO EAT FOOD FOR MANY OTHER REASONS THAN WHAT IT IS INTENDED TO DO, THAT IS TO FUEL OUR BODIES.

WITH THIS BOOK I WILL SHOW YOU PROVEN METHODS TO HELP YOU SUCCEED AS WELL AS HELP YOU RE-TRAIN YOUR THINKING SO THAT YOU WILL USE FOOD FOR JUST WHAT IT IS INTENDED FOR, TO FUEL YOUR BODY AND MIND.

FROM NOW ON WHEN YOU THINK OF FOOD, IT WILL BE TO HELP YOU FEEL BETTER, HAPPIER AND HEALTHIER! THE FOODS THAT YOU WILL CHOOSE WILL HAVE A POSITIVE IMPACT ON HOW YOUR BODY FUNCTIONS, WHICH IS WHAT YOU WANT. YOU CAN HAVE TREATS, BUT THAT IS WHAT THEY WILL BE – TREATS, NOT MEALS!

BY CHANGING YOUR THINKING AND YOUR LANGUAGE, YOU WILL CHANGE YOUR BODY AND FEEL HAPPIER, HEALTHIER AND SEXIER.

LET'S GET GOING AND CHANGE YOUR LIFE BECAUSE YOU ARE WORTH IT!

# ACKNOWLEDGMENTS

I want to acknowledge my husband, my partner and my best friend!
Thank you for allowing me the chance to do this and other things. Your
help and your belief in me has helped me grow. Thank you – I love you!

To my two boys – even though you did not always allow me to practice
on you, you are my greatest achievements! Just remember that you can
do anything you set your mind to!

A big thanks to all the people who helped me edit this book, and for
giving me your opinions and suggestions to make this book better for
others to achieve their goals. They are Tim Lindert, Sean Lindert, Kevin
Lindert, Carol Loeser, Tina Book, Heidi Calcagno, Letitia Huffstutler and
Peggy Greely. Thanks to anyone who I might have missed.

# CHAPTER 1

## *WHY THIS BOOK?*

Why this book?

I have helped thousands of people overcome bad habits with the use of hypnosis. I truly want to help every person that walks through my door and unfortunately there are not enough hours in the day to see everyone.

Sometimes a person will want to be hypnotized, but is too afraid because they do not know what hypnosis is. Sometimes a person does not have the money to come in to address a bad habit, like overeating. With that in mind, I decided to write a series of books to help those that really want to get the help. Now they can do it themselves, at a reasonable price.

This book offers you a chance to change and use the tools and techniques that work. You can either record your own hypnosis session, or you can use the MP3 associated with this book on my website. There are special access codes required which you will find in the book.

When you read the words and truly accept them, it will make the changes you want to happen faster. The reason for this is that you are now trusting and understanding exactly what will be said and incorporating the new behaviors that you want for your life.

With so many people having smart phones with the ability to record their own voices, you have the means to easily record a self-hypnosis session. You have the power in your hand to change that negative behavior, whether it is to quit smoking, lose weight, gain confidence, stop nail-biting, end the fear of flying, driving or improve test taking skills.

I have started to have some of my clients record their own changes. They are now giving the message to themselves and are becoming their own best friend. They have experienced changes faster now that they are in control, talking to the subconscious mind positively, calmly and with authority.

In this book you are not going to read personal stories as I will get right to the point, because you want to find out what to do and how to do it now! This is what you are going to get with this book---just plain and simple information for to use to meet and exceed your goals.

The scripts that are included in this book have been used to help people free themselves from their old habits. They are now living happier, healthier lives. You will be able to choose the scripts and suggested techniques to help you achieve the happiness and health that you desire.

Now is the time to take the next step – to do it. Once you read the scripts and see what it is you are to do, you will realize that it is not scary. Reading the scripts will make you feel better. Do it for you, for your health, for your future.

Remember, this is a gift to yourself for your future. Make it feel great and when it does, it will feel right, and when it feels right it becomes a part of you!

Now go and start changing and have a great life!

# CHAPTER 2

## *HOW TO USE THIS BOOK*

It's really very simple.

The first step is to acknowledge that you want to stop overeating and do what you need to do to let go of the weight.

You already know that you are not feeling good about yourself. Your clothes do not fit, your body hurts. You do not feel sexy. You just feel terrible about the way you let your body go.

The first step is to change your language. Everyone says, "I am going to lose the weight." This is the first problem. When you lose something you always look for it. For example, if you lose your keys, you look for them. From childhood, you have been programmed to look for the "thing" you lost, so your mind is now programmed to look for the weight you lost!

From now on you will say: "I am getting rid of the weight" or "I am letting the weight go" or even "the weight is gone for good because I do not need it any longer!" You could also say, "I am reducing my weight" or "I am getting fitter, trimmer and sexier!"

The other way I show people how to feed themselves is by thinking about a car. Your car is your vehicle that gets you places. You take good care of your car, because if you did not, you won't make it to work, school, or any place you want to go.

Let's take a look at your body. Your body is your vehicle. It takes you to work, school and places you want to go too. Yet most people take better care of their cars than they do their bodies.

If you were having a bad day you wouldn't drive up to the gas station and say "I am having a really bad day, so I want you to give me an extra $20.00 of gas for the car. It will make the car feel (run) better!" The gas attendant would look at you like you were crazy and proceed to tell you that the tank only holds so much gas and that the rest will spill over. You would have just wasted gas and money and nothing would have changed. It won't make the car run any better!

3

Now imagine that your stomach is your tank. It only holds so much food; about a fist full of food fits in the size of your stomach. So when you sit down and eat and eat and eat, the stomach takes what it needs and allows the rest of food to spill all over YOUR BODY! Again, nothing about the situation has changed and now you feel worse. You made yourself overeat and it did not help you one bit.

Let's stop the craziness and really change. As Albert Einstein once said, "If you keep on doing the same thing over and over and expect different results, that is insanity!"

Here is an outline to show you how you will now let the weight go…for good!

1.  Read the different opening scripts and choose the one you like best. This is going to help you to begin the process of relaxing. The more relaxed and calm you are, the easier it is to change. So choose one that makes you feel good while you are reading it. My most popular one is the first opening script.

2.  Next, choose 3 to 4 new behaviors that will replace your old behaviors. These new behaviors are what you want to start doing with your life now. There are plenty to choose from. If you do not like the wording, change it, make it yours and own it. Use positive words. You are not allowed to use the words in *Chapter Four, Words You Are Not Allowed to Use.* Instead, choose words that will inspire you. You will find those words in *Chapter Five, Your New Language.* These words will give you the inspiration you will need to see this through.

3.  Afterwards, choose a closing script to help you put together your hypnosis session.

4.  Choose calming music to play as you record your own session. Music has a wonderful effect on the mind and body. One of the things I recommend to my clients is to play music that is uplifting and makes you feel good or relaxed. Piano or guitar music works the best. I recommend George Winston, Jim Brickman, Kenny G, or music that helps you relax.

5.  Get it all together – even if you rip out the pages or copy them

down – so that everything is together and ready to record.

6.      Record your session. You can use your cell phone or even a computer that has a recording device in it. Speak to yourself as you would to a best friend or your loved ones. It might sound strange to you at first, hearing your own voice, but go with it. See how it feels to tell yourself to make the changes, to live free from the old habits that were dragging you down! Have fun with it. If you want, have someone record it for you--- maybe your kids, your spouse or someone that means a lot to you. This way you will hear them cheering you on and letting you know that they love you and believe in you! Do it! Pick a day and time to do it – don't wait another minute. You have already wasted so much of your time overeating and becoming unhealthy slowly – why wait? Even if you make today the day – do it. Pick a quiet room and record the scripts in a nice soothing voice and then listen to it that day and that night. In fact, I want you to listen to the recording at least 10 days in a row, preferably right before you go to bed. The reason why is because the last thing you think about, read, hear, see or do is what your mind works on. Let it be that you are a healthy eater for life! Either way – DO IT!

7.      Listen to your recording in a nice quiet place or before you go to bed. Your subconscious mind will do the rest.

8.      DO NOT LISTEN WHILE DRIVING!!!!

You will see and start to feel the changes happen - sometimes immediately, or over a few days. Don't give up! Own it, believe it and visualize you making the changes, and they will come. Occasionally, there will be times when you feel like you are out of control. In this book, I have included tools and techniques that will make you feel better, clear your mind and put you in control. Use these tools and record them so you will have them with you at all times! Trust me, they work.

Now, let's get to the good stuff! Turn the page and remember – this is your life, to create and to make it what you want. You are the author – this is your blank page – how are you going to write your future? Make it a good one and have fun!

# CHAPTER 3

## *WHAT IS HYPNOSIS REALLY LIKE?*

What is so fascinating about hypnosis is that you really are the one that allows it to happen. To have you understand what I am saying, let's say you wanted to stop feeling bad about your life. You could be upset about your weight, your bills, your love life or lack of a love life, smoking, nail biting---you get the picture.

With hypnosis, which is like guided imagery, you picture and see in your mind things happening differently, with solutions and new ways of behaving. You begin to feel good about these things, your body feels good and your mind and body want to continue to feel this way. In hypnosis, your subconscious mind is like your magic genie; your wish is its command. So, if you want to eat less, your subconscious mind starts to work on that. If you want to make more money, fall in love, be better in sports, anything that you are looking to change, hypnosis can help you get there.

If I told you that every day you experience some sort of hypnosis, would you believe me? Well you do. When you are driving your car, and singing, and you arrive at your destination without realizing you did, this is a form or hypnosis. When you are reading a book and are so into it that the outside world is not even there, this is hypnosis.

When you tell yourself that eating a piece of chocolate will relax you – this is hypnosis! Why? Because if you believe that the chocolate can relax you, your mind and body says "okay". Instead the sugar and carbs are being turned into unneeded, unwanted fat, because your body didn't need it to relax, so it now stores it as fat. In your mind you say, I needed this and now I am relaxed. The good feeling however lonely lasts for a moment. After that, you get angry at yourself for stuffing your face instead of dealing with the situation that created the stress, tension, anxiety, unhappiness, etc. Without evening knowing it, you have been hypnotized!

The big questions I always get regarding hypnosis are: "How will I feel?" and "You won't make me do something stupid?"

Well, here is how many people feel – some feel like they are just so heavy, while others feel that they are just floating, while others said they were very relaxed, and some even fell asleep.

Some people say they can hear what was being said, while others say they could sometimes hear the words, and yet others say that they heard nothing. Despite the differences, they were all hypnotized. There is no "right way" to feel. Each person has a different experience.

Now – can I make you do something you don't want to do? NO! Why? Simply, because if you do not want to do something, you won't do it. It really is that simple!

Why don't more people use hypnosis? It's because they are afraid.

Look at the way hypnosis has been explained to you - you lose control, you bark like a dog, you do stupid things. Well, first, that is stage hypnosis – and with stage hypnosis, the people going up on stage already know and accept that they are going to be made fools of, so to them it's all fun. With the medical or alternative medicine type of hypnosis, it is you that determines what is going to happen and how; so you are in control. Why wait? If you have been having issues and nothing else has seemed to work, give hypnosis a try.

Think about what you want out of life, or what is not happening, and how badly you want it. Don't get stuck or be afraid. As Bob Proctor said in the movie, **The Secret**, "You don't know how electricity works, and yet you use it." Use hypnosis and make change happen for you. Here is how your mind works.

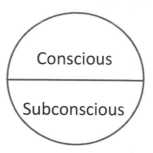

There are two parts to your mind: the conscious mind and the subconscious mind. Your conscious mind does all the learning, takes in all the information. Consciously, you can only pay attention to one thing at a time. Consciously, you are aware of the things that are going on around you. But consciously, you also have two voices – the good one and the bad one. The good one tells you that you can do things because you've got it. The bad voice tells you that you can't do something; it's no use, give up! When these two voices are fighting, you can never get anything done or you listen to the voice that is the loudest. So we don't play with the conscious part of the mind. There is no negotiating with your conscious mind.

There is also your subconscious mind. Your subconscious mind handles all your bodily functions. You don't directly think about breathing, your heart beating, or swallowing - it's all handled by your subconscious mind. Your subconscious mind also takes any thought, belief, action or reaction that you own in your mind and body and it says, "Your wish is my command."

If you think and say you cannot do something, your subconscious mind makes sure that it comes true. The subconscious mind doesn't argue; it just does.

Likewise, when you want to change for the better and you feel good and relaxed, your subconscious mind says, "Your wish is my command!" So that is why we play with the subconscious mind!

# CHAPTER 4

# *WORDS YOU ARE NOT ALLOWED TO USE TO DESCRIBE YOURSELF!*

The following words are now forbidden to be used when you are talking about yourself or to yourself! Why, you ask? The reason is that the following words are failure words. You will see what I mean.

**Try, can't, won't, would, could or should, and hope.** Here is why.

When a person says I will **try** to be there at 5 pm, you know that they won't.

The word **can't** – means you are correct – you **can't** do it! Period, you have given up!

The word **won't** – means you barely did it – it **won't** work – because it's in your mind that it will not work.

**Would, could or should** – watch your body when you say these words – see how it gives up. I **would** or I **could** – maybe I **should** – I don't know.

Again, you gave up.

**Lose** – If you lose it, you are programmed to find it. So no more lose. Instead you will **"get rid of the weight"**, or **"let go of the weight for good!"**

Now with the word **hope** – this is what people say. I **hope** it works.....that's real positive. They sound like they are defeated before they begin. Sometimes it is said in a positive way – but it always lacks confidence, so it is not allowed.

This rule is non-negotiable. No using these words. End of story!

If you catch yourself using these words – **STOP SPEAKING** and **REGROUP**! Start over again and say what you can and will do. In the beginning, it might feel as if you keep on having to catch yourself and start over again, but trust me, it is so worth it! You are worth it, so do it for you! Remember, this is your script that your mind listens to, make every word count!

If you have other failure words that you find yourself using, add them to this list in the space below. Again, I would love to hear from you on what you have added!

My web site is **www.advancedhypno.com** and my email is **hypnosisbykathy@gmail**.com. Email me and let me know.

# CHAPTER 5

# *YOUR NEW LANGUAGE!*

Your new language – this is how you are going to speak to yourself and about yourself!

These are the words you are to use for your script and to speak to yourself every day.

- **I can!**
- **I will!**
- **I want!**
- **I deserve!**
- **I desire!**
- **I am worth it!**
- **I believe in me!**
- **I am important!**
- **I have faith that this will work and I have faith in me!**

See how this feels when you say these out loud!

- **I can do this!**
- **I will be a non-smoker!**
- **I deserve to be healthy and free!**
- **I desire to be healthy!**
- **I believe in myself.**
- **I am important and I am worth it so I am doing this for me!**
- **I have faith in my abilities and now I am doing it!**

See how much more powerful and determined you feel? Isn't it amazing!

Change your language and your whole body will change as well. Write these words down and keep them in places that you will see them all the time: in your car, on your mirrors, in your office. It will make a difference.

Here are other words that will keep you moving ahead in meeting your goals and changing your behavior!  Use them every day!

- **Be the solution!**
- **Lead by example!**
- **Aspire!**
- **Create!**
- **The sky is the limit!**
- **Excel!**
- **Wisdom!**
- **Character!**
- **Dare to soar!**
- **Praise yourself!**
- **Be proud!**
- **Respect yourself!**
- **Appreciate who you are!**
- **Whatever it takes!**
- **I make the difference!**
- **Knowledge is power!**
- **Ultimate in performance!**
- **I ROCK!**
- **Value who you are!**
- **Innovate!**
- **Think BIG!**
- **Be enthusiastic!**
- **Preserver!**
- **Never QUIT on you!**
- **Celebrate! I celebrate me!**
- **Gratitude! I am grateful for all the things in my life!**
- **WATCH ME!!!**
- **Persistence!**
- **Inspire! I inspire myself!**
- **Powerful!  I am powerful!**
- **Empowered!  I am empowered!**
- **Motivate yourself! Make it happen!**
- **Be the bridge!**

- I have ambition!
- **Drive to succeed!!**
- **Endurance! I have the endurance to see this through!**
- **Move above and beyond!**
- **Commitment! I am committed to me!**
- **Dedication to my goal!**
- **Be proud of your accomplishments – big or small!**
- **REACH, SOAR, ACHIEVE AND SUCCEED!!!**
- **Discover you!**
- **Opportunities and possibilities are here for you to take! Shine! Courage! Strength! Confidence! I have a new attitude! I am a winner!**
- **I am letting go of the weight for good!**

You get the picture. Just by saying these words and believing in them, you will see a difference immediately in your attitude and desire!

I have left some space here for you to add your own positive words or sayings. Again, I would love to hear from you on what you have added!

My web site is **www.advancedhypno.com** and my email is **hypnosisbykathy@gmail**.com. Email me and let me know.

# CHAPTER 6

# *YOUR OPENING SCRIPTS!*

*General Notes Regarding an Opening Script: When reading any of the opening scripts, read it to yourself as if you are speaking to your best friend or a person you really care about – YOU! Remember it is okay to change the words and keep on going even if you make a mistake. I do it all the time and it still works! Just reread the word or sentence, mistakes are no big deal. If you want, you could also have another person, someone you really care about, record this for you as well. Even your kids can read parts of it to you; this way it really has more than one meaning.*

*Choose the one that fits you best. When recording, you can read it to yourself as a third person or change the "you" to "I". In order to help you relax even better, play soft relaxing music in the background. Music is known to help people relax, so use it for your benefit.*

## FIRST CHOICE OPENING SCRIPT

### <u>Total body relaxation: (This opening script is the one I use the most. It allows you to relax your whole body. Enjoy.)</u>

Take a nice deep breath and as you exhale, let all the stress, tension and any thoughts that are swirling around in your mind, let them all begin to just wind down, wind down, wind down, and relax. That's right. Now take in another nice easy breath and as you exhale, just know that you are safe, secure and supported, so you can and will allow your mind and body to really relax, release and let go. That's right, just let go. You are ready to make the changes you want, need and deserve. You are ready to be a healthy eater for life and it feels great. It's time to do it, so now you relax even better and deeper than ever before.

Starting from the top of your head, feel all the muscles going down the back of your head into your neck, just relaxing and releasing and letting go. Feel how good it is to let it all go. Now feel that relaxation going from your neck into your shoulders. Feel any stress, tension, anger, anything that you are holding onto on your shoulders – just brush it away, let it drop off of your shoulders and as you do that, feel your shoulders relaxing even deeper, deeper than ever before. Now feel that relaxation going from your shoulders all the way down your arms, feel it going down deeper – down deeper – down deeper relaxed, all the way down to your fingertips. See how wonderful it feels to allow your arms, hands, neck and shoulders to just relax.

Now from the back of your neck, feel all those muscles in your back, feel them going deeper and deeper and deeper relaxed. Remember you are safe and secure and supported so you can and will allow your back muscles to just really relax. It feels so good to let it all go.

Now feel that wonderful relaxation going from the top of your head into your forehead muscles, feel the forehead muscles, your eyebrows and your eyelids so very heavy, so comfortable and so relaxed. Your eyelids are so very, very heavy and because of that, your whole body continues to relax even deeper and deeper. Feel the wonderful relaxation going from your eyes into your jaw muscles, feel those muscles really relaxing, releasing and letting go. Now feel that relaxation going from your jaw muscles into your neck muscles, your chest muscles and your stomach muscles. Feel how very comfortable and relaxed your whole body is – just allow it to drift and float and relax even deeper. That's right. Now feel your hips relaxing, your thighs, your knees, your calves, your ankles, your feet and toes, all relaxing, releasing and letting go…it feels so good to let it all go. That's right.

You are allowing every muscle, cell, organ, even the hair on your body to just relax, release and let go. It feels so good to let it all go.

Now you are ready to make the changes that you want, that you deserve and desire. You are now ready to let go of the old habits and reactions that have hurt you, they have held you back and have not helped you. So let them go!

Just imagine or pretend that in front of you are 5 of the nicest softest steps, and as you take an easy step down, you will become more and more relaxed, even better than ever before. And when you reach the bottom step, you will be at the most special place in the whole wide world, just for you. Now this place can be any place at all or it might not be any place. It's where your mind brings you - that is where you are meant to be.

Starting now,

- 5 - going down deeper and deeper
- 4 - really relaxing
- 3 - feeling your whole body just relaxing and releasing and letting go
- 2 - feeling so good to just relax and
- 1 - there you are - at the most special place just for you.

Now that you are there, all the stress, the tension, the fears and worries, it all just bounces off and away, that's right, it all just bounces off and away from you.

Because you are ready to make the changes you want and deserve, you are ready to let go of the old ways that you thought and acted and reacted. They have not helped you, they have hurt you, and so you are ready to let them go. So as you are standing in your very special place, you see a beautiful fluffy white cloud coming towards you. Now this cloud is able to speak to you and it says, "Release up to me all the old ways, the old negative thoughts, the things that have hurt you, not helped you, let them go. Let go of the old pictures and old words; you do not need them so let them go!" And as you lie back in your very special place, you see black smoke coming out of your mind and body, and it is the old ways, the old reactions and actions. The negative words and thoughts are all being cleansed away, washed away from your mind and body. Let go of all the reasons why you ate unhealthy foods. They are not good for you, so you let them go. See the old excuses being wiped away, washed away, so you are cleansed. See the cloud wipe away, wash away the hurt, the pain, from your mind and body, and as that is happening you are free, cleansed from the past and ready to move forward with the wonderful new behaviors that you want and desire.

As you see the cloud wiping away, washing away the last of the black smoke, the sun bursts through and it sends a ray of sunlight down, disintegrating the cloud. Now feel the sun warming you, feel it giving you the power, the strength and energy of the sun. It feels wonderful to know that you can and will now make the changes easily and effortlessly. You will now allow all of the new and beneficial behaviors that are good for you to grow stronger and stronger in your mind and body and all of these new wonderful behaviors will now exercise a greater influence over your thoughts, your actions and your reactions. You now give yourself permission to allow these new behaviors to be a part of you, because you deserve it and now you believe in you---feeling great and proud that you are doing this for your life and your future.

(SEE CHAPTER 7, NEW BEHAVIORS, TO INSERT AS PART OF YOUR PERSONLIZED SCRIPT FOR THE BEHAVIORS THAT BEST FIT YOUR NEEDS.)

## SECOND CHOICE OPENING SCRIPT

### At the ocean induction: (Some people need to see in their minds where they are going, so this opening script helps you to imagine exactly where you are.  Enjoy!)

Now close your eyes and allow your mind and body to just start to relax, and as you take in a wonderful deep breath, feel all the stress and tension from the day just wind down, wind down and drift away.  That's right – let it go.

Because you are ready to make the changes that you want, you deserve and desire, you are allowing your mind and body to just relax. The more relaxed you are, the faster the changes happen. You are taking in another nice deep breath and as you exhale, let all the stress, the tension, anything and everything swirling around in your mind – just let it go - feel it leaving with that exhale.

And what I would like for you to do is just imagine or pretend that you see a wonderful path.  The path is surrounded by tall grass and as you start down the path, you hear the wonderful sound of the ocean.  It will take you 10 steps to get to the ocean and as you take each step, your mind and body relaxes even deeper, even deeper than before and when you reach the ocean, you feel so great, calm and relaxed.

Taking your first step,

- 10 - feeling your mind and muscles just relaxing, releasing and letting go
- 9 - feeling your hands and legs so very heavy, so comfortable and relaxed
- 8 - feeling your mind just emptying out all thoughts
- 7 - feeling the warmth from the sun on your head and allowing the warmth to just go down your body
- 6 - starting to smell the wonderful salt water and allowing your senses to enjoy the trip
- 5 - becoming more and more relaxed
- 4 - feeling your back relaxing and releasing and letting go
- 3 - feeling your shoulders just letting go, and anything you had been carrying on your shoulders, feel it drop away or

brush it away, you don't need it on the beach

- 2 - feeling so excited and so totally relaxed and
- 1 - There you are, at you own beautiful beach.

Now this beach is your own special beach, meaning that you can be alone if you want or you can have anyone join you, anyone at all. And when you are at your very special beach, you notice that all the stress, the tension, fears, worries, anything and everything that was weighing you down, it all just bounces off and away from you. That's right – it all just bounces off and away from you.

You now feel totally relaxed, and you know that you are safe, secure and supported, so you really let yourself go. Feel your mind and body just relaxing deeper and deeper and deeper relaxed.

On your special beach there are many things for you to see and do, but the most important thing that you will be doing is letting go of the bad habits. You do not want them, you do not need them and they have been holding you back, hurting you. So you are ready to let them go. As you walk along your beach, you see a wonderful fluffy white cloud. Now this cloud is going to help you to remove the old habits, the old negative voices and thoughts, as well as your old reactions.

Remember, they are hurting you so you are ready to just let them go. As the cloud comes closer, it is able to speak to you and it asks you to please allow it to wipe away and wash away, cleanse the old habits, beliefs, actions and reactions that you know are bad for you, so you agree to let them go. See the black smoke coming out of your mind and body, and the cloud, it wipes it away, washes it from your mind and body, removing the negative talk, the negative words, the negative behaviors, so you are feeling clean, free and ready to move on. Let the cloud remove all the excuses why you overate. See the cloud wipe away and wash away the hurt, the pain, and allow you to start to heal. This is your life, your story, how are you now going to write it? With freedom and strength, courage and confidence, or with passion, love and faith? Or will you have all of these as a part of you? Remember - this is your story, you get to write it and live it the way you want. So make it big!

As the cloud washes away and wipes away the last of the black smoke, you see the sun burst through and as it does, it disintegrates the cloud to the furthest parts of the universe. And now feel the sun giving you the power, the strength and energy of the sun, so that all of the new and wonderful behaviors that you want and need and desire will become a part of you easily and effortlessly. Because you want them and you know that they are good for you, you can and will let them exercise a greater and greater influence over your thoughts, your feelings and your actions.

Starting now with you first new behavior –

(SEE CHAPTER 7, NEW BEHAVIORS, TO INSERT AS PART OF YOUR PERSONLIZED SCRIPT FOR THE BEHAVIORS THAT BEST FIT YOUR NEEDS.)

## THIRD CHOICE OPENING SCRIPT

**Confusion induction: (Sometimes people have too many things that they think about so they never really relax. We use a story and words that sound the same to confuse you. It's a fun way of just tuning out and letting go!)**

Start by taking in a nice easy breath and sitting or lying down, it really does not matter---here, there or anywhere, just so long as you do it, because you have realized that you are ready to make changes to your life and your world. You are ready to just start to think about the things you do not want to think about. That's right, don't think about relaxing. Anyone can relax, and you might be able to relax if you really wanted to. And because you are so very smart, so intelligent, and you already know how to relax, you can do it whenever you are ready.

This reminds me of the story of Snow White and the Seven Dwarfs. She was so busy cleaning and cooking and feeding the animals that she never really got time to rest. And since she was so busy with everyone else, she made a bad judgment call by accepting an apple from an old ugly witch. That was not a good choice at all, but that was the way they decided to write that story, but not you. You're too smart for that. You know that you are aware of your surroundings and so you can just relax. You know your own house, so you might hear noises that you already recognize. Now as you lie or sit here, there or anywhere, and you hear the noises, you now know not to let them distract you---because no one knows you better then you know yourself. So you can just allow your fingers or feet or toes to start to feel relaxed and loose and limp. Feel that wonderful feeling going to your head and hair, that's right even hairs relax. Now think about your arms or your fingers or your toes, because they already know how to relax and let go, just like you feel your two hands and two ears relaxing. Because you are just letting your mind drift off and if a thought pops up – you say no – not now, knowing you can handle it later if you want. This is your story, so you get to know how to say no or know to say yes when the time is right.

Right now you realize that you are hearing words that sound the same but mean different things. You could if you really wanted to figure it all out, or you can just let go and have your two ears just hear what you hear, here, there or anywhere.

And as you feel your two hands relaxing even deeper too, you now just let it go. No need to try to figure out what is happening here, instead you just let go.

As you take in another easy breath, you now listen to the words that are spoken to you and you just feel your mind and body go down and down and down, like spokes on a wheel, feel your thoughts go round, and round till they just calm down. Drifting and floating down to that wonderful place of letting go, and when you are ready you will really let it go and relax.

Now you realize that you do not need to hear what is being said here to understand that you too can do what you need to do - to let go and relax.

When you are relaxed, feel your mind just letting go, getting ready to make the changes that you want here and now, and knowing that you will allow yourself to make the changes easily and effortlessly, as you sit or lie down, here, there or anywhere. It no longer matters to you and that feels great, knowing that you now know the way to no longer hold yourself back.

You are now ready to make the changes that you want and deserve; this is your story and you are now writing it with passion and strength and courage. That is right - courage, to make your life better healthier and happier. You are worth it and accept that you are important.

Just like in the story Snow White, she cleans out the house of the old cobwebs and dirt. It was not helping the dwarfs, it was hurting them, just like your old habits and reactions are hurting you – you are ready to clean them out. So I want you to imagine or pretend that right in front of you is a wonderful fluffy white cloud. Now this cloud can speak to you and its telling you that it wants to help you wash away, wipe away all the negative things you have been holding onto – the negative talk, the negative actions and reactions. Sweep up to the cloud all the reasons why you ate unhealthy foods; they have not helped you, so let them go. Clean out all the excuses - that's right, throw them away. Remember they are hurting you, not helping you so let them go, go up to the cloud, and as you relax, you see from your mind and body black smoke being released and the cloud is wiping it away, washing it from your mind and body so you are cleansed, free and feeling open, ready for the changes that you want and deserve because you are accepting that you are worth it. As the cloud continues to clean your mind and body, you are getting ready to change your life, and as the last of the dirt and smoke is wiped away, the sun bursts through and it disintegrates the cloud to the furthest parts of the universe, and you feel free – open and ready to make the changes that you want, that are good for you and that you now know you can and will do because you are worth it. Your life is worth it and it feels great!

Now the first new wonderful behavior that you can and will do is:

(SEE CHAPTER 7, NEW BEHAVIORS, TO INSERT AS PART OF YOUR PERSONLIZED SCRIPT FOR THE BEHAVIORS THAT BEST FIT YOUR NEEDS.)

# CHAPTER 7

## *NEW BEHAVIORS TO CHOOSE FROM*

Choices for your script: These are the scripts that I have used with my clients. Take the ones that you like that feel good both mentally and physically. I usually only recommend making three to four new changes, because with too many changes, you might get overwhelmed, and if they all do not work, you might think the hypnosis is not working.

In my private sessions, my clients make three to four changes, because that is all you really need. You will see that your habits are only used for certain situations – you are not doing things that are bad for you throughout your whole day – so we are replacing those bad habits with new good and beneficial ones. You only need a few to make the change. Pick the ones that feel the best and remember, you can always change them up. There is no reason why you cannot continue to make yourself more recordings. This is your life, your story, and you get to write it any way you wish! That is so empowering to realize and accept.

Now here are your choices – and remember you can change the words in order to fit your style. Just do not use words that are negative! See the list in Chapter 4. You can also change out "you" for "I".

**You are now your own best friend! (This is to replace the feeling of the food as your best friend, or the feeling that you are alone. You are not; you have the best person on your side – yourself!)**

I have decided to be my own best friend, to cheer myself on and to like myself, to forgive myself for the past and to pick myself up when needed. I now feed myself good positive words to keep my mind and body motivated! As my own best friend, I will now push myself to do the things that are good for me. Just like I would talk to my own best friend, I will encourage myself to not give up, to love myself and to keep on being strong. I now accept myself as being my own best friend and it feels great – because I will never let me down again. Being my own best friend means I am never alone. I now explore the world and discover who I am and am open to opportunities and possibilities – reaching, soaring, believing and achieving! That's the new me and I love that! As my best friend, I now know that I will be stronger than ever before. I will achieve my goals and I know I am worth it. It feels great, it feels right! I look better, feel better and sexier!

**There is no try (Remember, try is a failure word. It gives you the permission to give up! So no more Try!!)** – I no longer use the word try to help me get to my goals. Try is not good enough for me. Instead I will use words such as: I can, I will, I am worth it and I will do it! I now believe in myself, changing my attitude and my outlook on life. This is my goal, my vision and dream – and I own it!

**You now fuel your body like a car- (When you pull up to the gas station and you are having a bad day you don't say, let's put in an extra $50.00 in the gas tank. If you did it would spill all over. That is what you did to your body. Not anymore.)**

You are now fueling your body like you fuel your car. You now fuel your body with good healthy and nutritious foods. The foods you now feed your body help to maintain good levels of energy, strength and endurance. Your body now uses the food as fuel and your metabolism is running perfectly. You feel great because now you are burning the unwanted fat from your body, looking and feeling better, happier, healthier and sexy! That's you and you love it!

Your body now requires fruits, vegetables, proteins and healthy carbs. Your body utilizes the healthy foods faster and you feel the difference in your body and mind.

**Your stomach – the size of your fist! (Your stomach is about the size of your fist. The more food you put in your stomach, the bigger it grows. However it has the ability to go back to its normal size.)**

You now acknowledge that your stomach is the size of your fist and that you only need to fuel your body with an amount of food that is the size of your fist. You now fuel your body 5 times a day – eating the correct amount of food, feeling energized and strong. Because you are eating the proper amount for your body, the unwanted and unneeded fat just melts away – off of your body.

You are taking great care of your body and it feels great! It feels amazing!

**You no longer eat after 8 pm- (After 8 pm your body is getting ready to sleep. The food you have eaten after 8 pm just turns to fat because it is not being used. No longer will you eat after 8 pm!)**

You have made a choice to no longer eat after 8 pm. Your body does not need it. Your body is getting ready to sleep and if you eat after 8pm, the food just sits there turning to fat. So no more eating after 8pm. If you feel hungry – you will either make a wonderful soothing cup of tea, drink water or seltzer, allow the liquids to help refresh your mind and body, feeling the warmth or coolness of the drinks sooth you, relax you, so you are satisfied and content. So no more eating after 8pm. You feel great and you are allowing your body to start the process of getting ready for a great night's sleep, doing what is best for your mind and body.

**Treats – (It is a treat – plain and simple -- not a meal, not something to make you feel better. It is a treat, so treat it that way!)**

When you want a treat, you now will take two bites and feel satisfied and content. You now understand that your body only wants a taste and you do exactly that--- a taste. You chew the treat slowly, allowing the taste and flavors to give your mouth all it needs. You are proud of yourself that you are taking great care of your body, eating the right amount and knowing that you are doing well and staying on track.

**Chew your food – (Most people do not chew their food more than three times before they swallow. By doing this, you are not allowing the mouth and stomach to do their jobs properly. Plus, it takes your stomach a longer time to register the food, causing you to overeat. Chewing allows the mouth, the body and the stomach to start the process of digesting and allows you to feel fuller faster. So chew your food more than three times!)**

You now chew your food at least 8 to 10 times. When you chew your food, you feel your mouth, stomach and mind all working together. Chewing your food allows the mouth to start the process of breaking down the foods, while satisfying your desires for the wonderful food. Chewing your food 8 to 10 times also allows your stomach to tell your mind when you are done. So when you are finished, you are finished. You now enjoy eating because you now taste the foods.

### Eating out – (Restaurants serve large portions that you do not need. Just because it is on your plate, does not mean you need to eat it!)

When you are dining out, you will either choose to share a meal or you will automatically eat half the portion. Asking for a doggie bag, you will save the other portion for the next day. You know that you do not need all the food the restaurant gives you and if you were to eat it all, you would feel sluggish and bloated. You also tell the waiter to skip the bread. You do not want to fill up on bread, wasting a wonderful meal. So there is no bread---you don't want it or need it. You are proud that you will eat the right amount of food for your body's needs and that you will be able to have it again to enjoy the next day.

### Alcoholic beverages- (Alcohol has no nutritional value and has many calories. Just watch what you drink and how much. Ask yourself, is it really worth the extra weight?)

When you want an alcoholic drink, you will have one drink. The drink is there to allow you to relax and enjoy the taste of the drink. You sip your drink, enjoying the taste, the smooth feeling of the alcohol on your tongue, just allowing your mind and body to relax. When you are done, you are done. You then reach for water--- wonderful, refreshing water---knowing you are doing this for your mind and body and feeling great!

### Food is not a friend – (Food fuels your mind and body. Food is there to help you feel balanced and whole. You now choose foods that help you succeed and not bring you down.)

No longer are you using food to help you get through stress, tension, sadness, loneliness, or for any other reason. Food is a fuel. You now choose good healthy foods to keep your mind and body working at their best. Food helps you to stay alert and focused. The food that you now choose will also help you to melt the unwanted fat away from your body because you are now utilizing the food you are eating; your body can and will burn the unnecessary fat away. You now enjoy knowing that food is here to help you feel and act better. You treat food as it is meant to be, as a fuel, and it feels great!

## Water – wonderful cleansing water. (Use this script to help you to replace your old habit of overeating and to give your body a chance to cleanse itself. You will feel much healthier when you drink water every day. )

Every day, I will drink wonderful, refreshing, renewing water. Water helps to remove the fat from my body. Water refreshes and renews my mind and body and skin. Water helps me to feel alive. When I drink water, I feel good, calm and relaxed. So I make sure that I am drinking 4 to 6 glasses of water a day to help me feel and act calmer, cleansed, refreshed and alive. I drink water because my body loves it and needs it. Water - I love it and I feel great! Wonderful cleansing water - I now drink it every day.

## Giving yourself a break from the moment. (This replaces the old habit of grabbing something to eat when you feel stressed, anxious and need to do something. Choose this healthy way to handle the stress.)

When life starts to get overwhelming, I will now get up and take a quick walk. Walking will help me to clear my mind and help my body get rid of the stress, the tension and the negative feelings. Walking allows me to breathe, to take a moment and to regroup. When I walk, whether it's down the hall, around the building, anywhere, I am feeling better and relaxed because I have chosen to do something healthy for my mind and body. I am proud that I am taking a break just for me, because I realize I am worth it.

## Walking for my health – as exercise. (This will help you to let go of the stress from the day but it also helps to build up your lungs and your health. Remember to check with a doctor before you do any exercises. )

From now on, I will walk at least 3 days a week - for me. I will make time to walk in the (choose your times and days – the more definite you are the better it works - morning, afternoon, evening) on these days (pick your three days or more) for at least 15 to 30 minutes, increasing the time and distance as I become healthier, fitter, trimmer and sexier!

I now love to walk, because when I walk I get to see nature at its best – seeing the changes in the scenery, enjoying walking by myself or with others (even with my dog/dogs.) When I walk, I feel great, alive and free. I am breathing better and using my muscles to grow stronger, fitter, trimmer and sexier. I also feel the fat leaving my body, because when I am walking, I am energized. Walking helps me to clear out my brain and any issues or problems that I had seem to go away with my walking.

I make time to walk for me, my health, and my family. Walking is important to me and I am important, so I make the time to walk, and it feels great! I am seeing the difference walking has on my life, my body and my thoughts – I love it!

**Exercising for me! (This will help you to let go of the stress from the day – but also helps to build up your stamina and increases your metabolism. Remember to check with a doctor before you do any exercises. )**

I am now exercising for me, choosing to exercise to help me become stronger, fitter, trimmer, healthier and definitely sexier. I exercise to make me feel better and I will do what I can to build up my strength and endurance because I am worth it.

I now will start out exercising 3 days a week (choose your days – it is important to do this because you are making a commitment – so choose your days), starting out for 15 to 30 minutes, feeling my body growing stronger each and every time. I will do weights, treadmill, elliptical, yoga, Pilates, dancing, jumping rope, anything that gets my body moving! I enjoy the change that is happening to my body. I am looking forward to feeling energized and more in tune with my body – alive and definitely sexier. I am looking forward to wearing new clothes

When I work out I also feel all the stress and tension from the day just melt away. My mind is clearer and I also find solutions to challenges when I work out, because as I work out, my mind is clear from the stress and tension of the day.

The more I work out, the more I feel confident in myself. I like myself and I am proud that I am doing great things for my body. I will reach, soar, achieve and succeed!

**Walking to relax – (This is a shorter version of the other walking suggestion and is to be used if you just want to clear your mind and get out and enjoy. Again, you should check with a doctor before exercising.)**

You have made a decision to walk. Walking really helps you to clear your mind, enjoy the sights and sounds of nature, and just makes your body feel alive. You will now walk 3 to 4 days a week (again, choose your days and times to walk), starting out for 15 to 30 minutes each time, and as you get stronger and fitter, you can and will increase your time and days. You really enjoy the walk. When you walk, allow anything that was bothering you to just melt away. As you walk, you feel your muscles growing stronger and healthier and you feel sexier too! As you walk, you feel the fat also melting away and it feels great! You make the time to walk; you feel more calm, confident and in control.

**Two deep breaths. (This technique helps to replace the way you felt when stressed and looking for food. The way you breathe in this exercise will help you to increase your oxygen level and you will feel much more relaxed. )**

From now on, any time you feel stressed, tense, sad, angry or overwhelmed, or have a craving or just need to release all the thoughts swirling around in your head, you will now take a nice, deep breath in through your nose, and as you exhale out from your mouth, all of the stress, tension, fears, worries, anything and everything that was bothering you, is now exhaled out of your mind and body. That's right, just let it go, feel it leaving your mind and body.

You then take in another nice deep breath through your nose and as you exhale out from your mouth, you now feel calm, relaxed, confident and in control, knowing that you can and will handle the situation calmly, confidently and in control, feeling so much better than ever before and proud that you are clear thinking and in control.

**Three Finger Release. (I usually recommend that you use your dominate hand. When you are touching or rubbing your three fingers together, you will need to think about your favorite color and your favorite number. If you do not have one, think about a color that makes you feel good and a number that means something special to you. Also chose three fingers on your hand that you can touch together, for example, your thumb, pointer finger and middle finger.)**

Take in a nice, easy breath and as you exhale, touch your three fingers together; feel how nice and comfortable they feel touching each other. Take in another nice, easy breath and as you exhale, start to think about your favorite color and as you think about your favorite color, think about all the reasons why you like it. When you see this color it makes you feel good, calm, happy and alive. As you think about your color, feel how your mind and body are relaxing and letting go. Now take in another nice, easy breath and as you exhale, think about your favorite number – think about why you like this number and all the wonderful meanings this number has for you. As you think about your favorite number, see how much better you are feeling. Your mind and body are relaxing and you are now clear thinking. As you touch your three fingers together, you will now remember your favorite color and number and automatically and instinctively, you become calm and relaxed. Now you can take a moment or two to just allow this feeling to become a part of you. You now can and will be able to handle any situation calmly, confidently, and you are in control of your thoughts and emotions. Any time you want to relax, you will touch your three fingers together and it will happen automatically and instinctively, feeling great – calm, relaxed and in control. You can use this anytime and anywhere and each time you do, you feel better and better and you love it!

**Music, sweet music!   ( I have my clients use this in their car to help them to relax and to realize that songs and singing are a lot more fun than just sitting in traffic and eating! )**

Now every time you are driving in your car, you listen to music that helps to relax you, energize you, to help you get through the drive feeling better, happier and now healthier. When you are driving, you are listening to the music, hearing the words – the meaning of each song - singing and even moving to the music, listening to songs that come from the heart or songs that remind of you of times that made you feel alive!  Music has a wonderful way of changing your moods, so you now will make your music list and have it with you to keep you happy and healthy on the way home.  You are breathing better because you are singing and using your lungs, moving a bit in your car, keeping your drive fun!  And the best part of this is that you can have more than one list for your ride.  Listening to music lifts you up and you really love it!

**Your guardian angel – (I use this to let people know that you do have angels or spirits around you helping you all the time. If you know you have a guardian angel, use him or her.  If not, just sit quietly for a moment and see or feel if you have one or more. Then you can even ask them their names.)**

From now on, you feel your guardian angel helping you, guiding you and keeping you strong.  You now know that you can lean on your guardian angel in times of need and you can talk to him/her when you are frustrated, angry or just in the need of help. The guardian angel will help you to become more confident, grow in strength and endurance and feel so much more positive and powerful with your goal. Your guardian angel loves you and is there always for you. When you need to feel safe, your guardian angel will wrap its wings around you, so you feel and are safe and secure.  It feels great that you are now never alone.

## You are a champion! (I use this for those that like to know that when there is a challenge, they are up for the task. People that like sports or competitions like this one. Go for it!)

You are now being the champion that you already know you are! Champions never give up and you are not giving up on you and your goals! You recognize that there will be hurdles and things that will "try" to block you, but you are a champion and there is no "try" – there is only achieving. You are now doing everything in your power to reach, to soar and to achieve whatever goals you want, and it feels amazing that you are doing it for you, for your life and for your future.

## Keeping your mouth busy – (I use this for those that want to keep their mouths or hands busy.)

Anytime you want to keep your mouth or hands busy, you now choose to either enjoy a great piece of gum or play with a toothpick. As you are chewing the gum, you now notice how the flavors are so much stronger than ever before and you enjoy the refreshing taste the gum gives you. Your mouth feels refreshed and you like the tingling on your tongue from the flavors of the gum.

Or if you want to keep your hands and mouth busy, you now choose a toothpick to occupy you for a minute or two. You have fun twirling the toothpick from one place to another, just having fun playing with the toothpick. After a minute or two you are done, finished, and you throw it away.

# CHAPTER 8

# *CLOSING SCRIPTS*

Closing scripts: This is how you will end your personal session. Again, you can change the words to fit your own style. You can either use the word "you" or "I" when you record your session

## FIRST CHOICE OF A CLOSING SCRIPT:

So now that you have accepted all these wonderful new changes that you want, that you deserve and know are good for you, you are now ready to have them be a part of you. These new behaviors will become a part of you now and forever. You realize that you are important and that you want these new wonderful behaviors, that you deserve them, desire them and that you make them a part of you easily and effortlessly. Now say to yourself: I want them and I allow them to be a part of me. I own these changes and new behaviors and it feels great!

It feels amazing to know I am now going to change, for me, for my life and my future. I love it.

In a moment I will count from three to one, feeling better than ever before and excited for all the new changes to take place for the rest of my life.

Three (3)...Really enjoying the last few moments of this wonderful, relaxing recording.

Two (2)...Accepting and believing in myself to make the changes easily and effortlessly because I am worth it, remembering that I have people who love me and want me to be happier, healthier, and to be around. Because of that, I will do these new behaviors and allow them to be a part of me for all of us - because we are all worth it.

And one (1)...If it is time to go to sleep, I will roll over and go into a peaceful sleep, sleeping through the night and having great dreams, and allowing my mind and body to rest, to relax and to rejuvenate. While I sleep, my body renews and heals so when I wake up, I will feel happier, healthier and ready to face the day, remembering that each day is my gift, a present for me to open, to discover, explore and embrace.

But if it is time for me to wake up, I will feel like I took a wonderful nap, ready to face the day – again remembering that each day is a gift.

And 1...Either roll over and go to sleep or welcome back!

## SECOND CHOICE FOR A CLOSING SCRIPT:

I am ready to accept and own these new wonderful ways of behaving, now and forever. I am ready to make the changes that I want and deserve, for myself and for my future!

These new behaviors will become a part of me easily and effortlessly. I am making this a part of me now and for life!

I see myself acting in these new ways and loving the way that I feel, act and behave. I feel and act differently now because it is good for me. I love myself enough to make this happen – not only for me – but for those I love as well. My future belongs to me and I am now taking control and changing. It feels great that I have made this decision and now I am doing it.

In a minute I will count from three to one…feeling so much better than before and knowing that changes are happening now and forever…reaching, soaring, achieving and succeeding! That's what I do now and forever!

Three (3)…Really enjoying the last few moments of this wonderful relaxing recording.

Two (2)…Feeling my hands, feet, body moving and feeling great, so very relaxed and ready to go.

And One (1)… Eyes open and welcome back.

# CHAPTER 9

# *OTHER COOL TRICKS TO DO!*

## THE FIST TRICK – TO LET GO OF THE STRESS OR CRAVING.

We are going to play a game. It's going to be a fun game and the game is to get you to be free---free from your thoughts. So any time that you think you need unhealthy foods or to overeat, what I would like for you to do is the following.

I would like you to take your right hand and pretend or imagine that whatever emotion, feeling, or craving that you have for the unnecessary food, you will place it in your right hand. Close your eyes and make a fist. Start squeezing your fist really hard! Counting to five, while squeezing your fist, say out loud:

- **1 - I'm bigger than this emotion or craving!**
- **2 - I'm stronger. I don't need it!**
- **3 - I think it makes me feel better but it's making me fat and ugly and I don't want to look or feel this way!**
- **4 - I will not allow this to control me!**
- **5 – I am letting this feeling go!**

When you are done, open up your hand and think about what you had for breakfast or what you did not have!

And then in your left hand, take something that makes you feel really good. It should be an experience, a memory. It could have been a joke, a good movie. It could have been a vacation, maybe a wedding, a birth of a child, a graduation, maybe even a promotion.

Place that memory in your left hand and as you do, close your eyes, make a fist and start to squeeze your fist really hard. Then say out loud the memory that makes you feel great while counting to five. For example:

- **1 - Thinking about the joy,**
- **2 - The love, the peace, the happiness,**
- **3 - The health, the laughter, the smiles,**
- **4 - Anything and everything about that memory that made**

**you feel good,**

- **5 – Feeling so good and proud that you are in control.**

When you are done, open your fist and think about what you had or are having for lunch. **Then just close your fists close your eyes and just start counting to 5, squeezing as hard as you can…1, 2, 3, 4 and 5.**

When you open up your eyes, you're going to realize you have no need, no desire, no craving for the unhealthy food. That's right. It's gone. That's how simple this technique works.

## OVER EATING WORKSHEET

Pinpointing when, where, and why you overeat.

The following exercise will help you to analyze your eating pattern, to identify when you are most likely to overeat.

When – I overeat when I am feeling:

| | |
|---|---|
| Lonely | YES___ NO___ |
| Isolated | YES___ NO___ |
| Ignored | YES___ NO___ |
| Unhappy | YES___ NO___ |
| Stressed | YES___ NO___ |
| Insecure | YES___ NO___ |
| Awkward | YES___ NO___ |
| Uncomfortable | YES___ NO___ |
| Unimportant | YES___ NO___ |
| OTHER_____ | YES___ NO___ |

Where – I overeat:

| | |
|---|---|
| In the car | YES___ NO___ |
| In front of the TV | YES___ NO___ |
| During large gatherings | YES___ NO___ |
| At my home or other people's homes | YES___ NO___ |
| Outside of work with my co-workers | YES___ NO___ |
| With friends | YES___ NO___ |
| At a restaurant or bar | YES___ NO___ |
| At social events | YES___ NO___ |
| Other_____ | YES___ NO___ |

Why – I overeat whenever I need:

| | |
|---|---|
| Companionship | YES___ NO___ |
| A break in the routine | YES___ NO___ |
| Comfort | YES___ NO___ |
| Relaxation | YES___ NO___ |
| To control my feelings/emotions | YES ___ NO___ |
| To not feel left out | YES___ NO___ |
| To look occupied | YES___ NO___ |
| Other_____ | YES___ NO___ |

After you have pinpointed the times, locations, and reasons you overeat, you can begin to change your behavior patterns. Look back at the WHEN category. Which ones are marked "YES?" In the chart below, under the WHEN heading, write, "I overeat when I am feeling (isolated, stressed, uncomfortable and so on)." Follow the same procedure for the WHERE and WHY categories. Now you should have three or more statements that ring true for you.

WHEN_____NEW BEHAVIOR_____

WHERE_____NEW BEHAVIOR_____

WHY_____NEW BEHAVIOR_____

# CHAPTER 10

## *WHY I BECAME A HYPNOTIST*

I would like to tell you a little bit about myself. I was a mortgage banker with my own company and was very successful. I had a great career that let me meet people of all different lifestyles. I had to travel for work and that is when my issue started. Why? I started to have panic attacks when I was driving over bridges. I live in New Jersey and there are bridges everywhere! My panic attacks became so bad that I would physically get sick, to the point where I would throw up! As I was driving over the bridge I felt like I was going to pass out. It was definitely not fun.

Needless to say, this hampered my ability to see clients. If I had to cross a bridge to see you, most likely we never met in person. This was a silent torture that I lived with; no one really knew I had this fear. It was embarrassing. I was this strong successful business woman who would become this pathetic crying baby because of a bridge and it wasn't just bridges over water, no, that would be too easy. It was any kind of a bridge - an overpass, small or large bridge, size did not matter. What's worse, the panic attacks started to happen in tunnels as well. It was terrible.

Around this time, a close family member started to have fears and was diagnosed with OCD, Obsessive Compulsive Disorder. We all tried to help this family member out, whether it was with therapy, medicines, diets, vitamins, bio-feedback, you name it, it was considered and tried. Nothing helped, because we were not getting to the root of the problem.

One night at two o'clock in the morning when I couldn't sleep, I happened to pick up a copy of **Prevention Magazine** and in that issue was an article about how hypnosis helps with fears and phobias! The article showed how hypnosis was helping people get over their fears and phobias in a few sessions and I was sold! This was my "aha" moment! I knew that I had found my answer - not only for myself, but for the family member as well.

I was so excited that I went to my office and started to look up hypnosis schools. The reason I wanted to go to school was that I wanted to learn why this worked, how it worked, and I wanted to be in control. Let's face it - the word "hypnosis" has a scary association with losing control or even mind control. So my thought was, let me learn how it is done, how to do it, so I can control it and so no one can control me.

After a discussion with my husband, I signed up for the classes. They were on the weekends and I had two small children at home. I knew I would be gone from 8 AM to 5 PM, so I needed my family on board with this as well. My husband agreed and off I went.

Well, needless to say, I had a great time. I learned so much. One of the most important things I learned was that you don't lose control; if you do not want to be hypnotized, you won't be hypnotized. I volunteered to be the genuine pig most of the time, because I wanted to experience the feeling and be able to understand it better. I also wanted to see if the changes really could happen and most of the time they did. Hypnosis is not an exact science, so sometimes if you don't want to change or don't like the change, you will not let it happen. This experience not only happened with me, but with the 19 other students in the class. And what I realized was that if I really wanted something to happen or to change, it did, because I wanted it to happen.

I have helped people stop smoking, lose weight, gain the confidence they need to drive, to pass tests, have bathroom control, have better sex and be better at sports.

I have also dealt with sleep issues, getting over love, pain; you name it, I have probably seen it or heard about it.

If you want to contact me, my email is **hypnosisbykathy@gmail.com** or **www.advancedhypno.com**. I always love to hear from my clients on how they are doing and I would love to hear from you as well.

# CHAPTER 11

# *HYPNOSIS HELPS IN THESE AREAS*

Hypnosis can also help in these areas:

o      ADD/ADHD
o      Bedwetting
o      Better Golf
o      Concentration
o      Depression
o      Fears
o      Migraines
o      Motivation
o      Obsessive Compulsive Issues
o      Pain Management
o      Panic Attacks
o      Public Speaking
o      Relationship Building
o      Sales Improvement
o      Self Confidence
o      Sexual Dysfunction
o      Sleep Issues
o      Smoking Cessation
o      Sports Improvement
o      Stress Reduction
o      Study Skills
o      Test Taking
o      Tinnitus
o      Weight Loss

# CHAPTER 12

# *YOUR FREE WEIGHT REDUCTION MP3*

If you want a free Weight Reduction MP3, please go to **www.advancedhypno.com** to the free MP3 section and type in the words "foodisfuel".

You will get a full session of a Weight Reduction MP3 for your use.

# REFERENCES

Feldman, J. The Institute of Hypnosis. (2005) *Hypnoscripts -137 Hypnotherapy and Induction Scripts.* Manalapan, NJ.

Ellner, M. Fist Trick – Conference Call around 2007/2008 – New York

Havens, R.A. & Walters, C. (1989) *Hypnotherapy Scripts: A Neo-Ericksonian Approach to Persuasive Healing.* New York: Brunner/Mazel Publishers

13208992R00031

Made in the USA
San Bernardino, CA
14 July 2014